Also by Toni Thomas:

Chosen
Fast as Lightening
Walking on Water
Blue Halo
Ace Raider of the Unfathomable Universe
You'll be Fast as Lightning Coveting my Painted Tail
Hotsy Totsy Ballroom
Love Adrift in the City of Stars
In the Pink Arms of the City
In the Kingdom of Longing
The Things We Don't Know
In the Boarding House for Unclaimed Girls
They Became Wing Perfect and Flew
Unburdened Kisses
Bandits Come and Remove Her Body in the Night
There is This
Here
The Smooth White Vanishing
Perishing in the Rain
A Different Measure of Moonlight
The Secret Language of River
Inside Her a River of Snow was Traveling
The Arbiter of Her Own Flame
Paradise on a Shoestring
A Bride of Amazement
A Portuguese Lullaby is What I am After
In the Hermitage of the Soul
You can Cast Around Forever in my Father's Shoes

In the Patron Saint's Daybook

Published 2025
Annalese Press
West Yorkshire HD9 3XZ
England

Copyright © 2025 Toni Thomas

All rights reserved. No part of this publication may be reproduced, stored, or transmitted in any form, or by any means electronic, mechanical or photocopying, recording or otherwise, without the express written permission of the publisher.

Design, layout and illustrations by
Peter Wadsworth
Cover: Fresco of St Columbanus, Brugnato Cathedral

British Library Cataloguing-in-Publication Data
A catalogue record for this book is available on request from the British Library.

ISBN 978-1-0685744-7-4

Contents

Part One - *In the Beginning*

In the beginning	3
The girl carries water	4
First we promised you weight	5
My mother told me	6
Worship came wearing	7
In the patron saint's pocket	8
Some people poked fun	9
Sometimes words escape me	10
We wanted to storm the summit	11
Someone claimed my prayers	12
In the contemptuous midnight	13
You are weighing things	14
In the dark	15
In the territory of loss	16
Can we always count on luck	17
We had been courting	18
Back then	19

Part Two - *What does the Dark Dream*

What does the dark dream	23
We are picnicking	24
When my children attempted to banish	25

He calls me *flimsy*	26
The man upstairs	27
The boy down the block	29
When the birds came	30
I'd heard the queen of media talking	31
Enquiry from the Rock Quarry Foundation	32
You are dealing cards	34
I practiced my penmanship	35
When the patron saint of invisible places	36
When the rain comes	37
He is counting up	38
Something courses through my life	39
Who impels the sun	40
Who climbs the trellis	41

Part Three - *In the Country of My Longing*

The plaudits of my heart	45
The hours	46
I am peeling things loose	47
My mother is wearing	48
I can imagine you	49
I want to see you tonight	50
Let me remember you	51
Who causes the cock to still	52
If I woo you with poems	53
In the country of my longing	54
What if fire drives the sledge	55
The patron saint of fallen means	56

Was I awe struck	57
When I call your name	58
What will the night bring	59
Your dark is a shower of stars	60

Part Four - *A Mistress of Stolen Vows*

I have heard	65
Voices	66
Out back	67
When I wear down my browns	68
It isn't the first time	69
If restlessness	70
You carry the weight of sorrow	71
I bless your hands	72
In the notebook	73
Who makes for beauty	74
The night is a mistress of stolen vows	75
When the dark	76
I thought of you yesterday	77
In the book of the patron saint of wonders	78
It would be a mistake	79
They are playing boules	81
This day	82
You persist	83
When I come	84
Hear my plea	85
I cast out my kisses	86
I tell you about my history	87

Fashion me one of your nosegays	88
When the merchants came	89
When the patron saint of miracles slips in	90
When you arrive	91
What can I say	92
No one said I was destined for aerial	93

Part Five - *Three Parts Flame*

You are solar powered	96
I'm not sure	97
When we move from here	98
You might think	99
You came to me	100
You are crushing cardamom	101
Year after year	102
Without fork or spoon	103
In the patron saint's daybook	104
On a clear day, at a certain hour	105
When your shoes rise out of the closet	106
When you peek into your soul	107
When I worship you	108
When I arrive inside	109
Have you come	110
Listen	111
To eat cake with a saint	112
When the cottonwoods arrived	113
We have seen the glow	114
Today the patron saint of favors arrived	115

They say it takes centuries	116
Now that the wind has hushed	117
Maybe	118
We called into the future	119
We cut the ribbon	120
Color blind this love	121
Pasha	122
In the field	123

Trees were my teachers
melodious trees
and i learned to love
among the flowers.
I grew up in the arms of the gods.
                    Friedrich Hölderlin

My soul was a little blue dress
the color of the sky;
I left it on a rock by the sea
and naked I came to you,
looking like a woman.
                    Edith Södergran

*In the language of saviors
will you travel me anywhere
even in a wounded tide*

*see what I see
beyond the despair?*

Part One

In the Beginning

In the beginning

my mother wore the world
in her robe
kisses marked no territory
were meant to be squandered
and the light
and the light
it bore a hole in my soul
stunned the day with seagulls.

In the beginning
the wind never traveled blind
we gathered deadfall
wiped the dark with our lips
didn't need to steal peaches
check our look in the mirror.

In the beginning I was enough
and the world was enough.
We didn't just beg our supper
we sang.

The girl carries water

is young, in love with mud
spring dresses
limbs seeded in séance and fleece
nights that call her name
offer up the sea's rock salt.

No one has yet tempted her
with the poisonous apple
trained her to act smart
jar midnight
drown the dreams
in her pocket.

The girl carries water
promises to shade
make your body into a fruited bush
place where the blind see
every act of faith holds a fountain.

How many times has she called
your name out of the blue forest
coaxed the clouds of the dark
to bring snow?

First we promised you weight

ecclesiastics
the aerial of lift
promised combed words
to brush diligent.

When the dark set in
you allowed it
when the day wore a stable of kisses
you grinned.

It was hard having so many choices
figuring things out
separating the pallbearer's uniform
from the cradle.

First we promised no catastrophes
that the eye of the storm
would stay decent.
Later we learned to snip thread
name call
watch the night get buried
in bug spray
to stay clean.

My mother told me

silence presses its own hankies
not every flower needs a name

told me the things I like best
might fold here
the forest holds a colony
of shy voices.

It was the age of answers.
We stuffed them in our seams
our marriage, discontents
till they grew hard as marbles
harbored a delusional landscape
intractable ledge.

I began to answer in basalt.
Ate rocks till my mouth bled.

Worship came wearing

its starched collar
patent leather shoes
as if the day
is a crisp prayer book
the voice holds no pins.

Worship came wearing
its menace and wise
salty inebriations
where god is a lamppost
never lecherous.

But what will I do
when the ordinary sermon
deserts me
its lemon icing
contrite shoes

what will I do when want
unbuttons her blouse
the moon paws sexy?

In the patron saint's pocket

you'll find a miniature prayer book
sketch of the sky
burdock and gull feather
crumbs of a cracker
hole where things slipped through
became lost.

In the patron saint's pocket
my name is sewn in the seam
the stub of a pencil tracks want
treachery
the small joy of swallows
torch of sunset.

But still messages arrive crimped
my voice carries crease
a pitted ocean
half lit flame.

Some people poked fun

pronounced me as pie eyed
warned that the night runs on seams
not every answer is a cymbal.

I grew quiet after that
set to store my treasure
in hidden mounds.

How contentious the world can be
starched and color coded
made to act smart
in a field of weed.

Sometimes words escape me

their inky inlets
unearned celebrity
the night speaks forensic
a continent of lost doves
orphaned prayer book.

Sometimes my country eludes me
its mortuaries
blue thirst, neon
I carry stones
want to build you a well

offer up water
a place where
even stolen kisses
find a home.

We wanted to storm the summit

plant a flag of our own
one with ten stripes
sewn from scrapes of bathrobe
a skull, stardust
wanted to stay valiant
crusaders of a cause
missionary outpost
where every insurgence
holds rule.

We stormed as we ached
pummeled then wept
till the ground bled a deathbed
only one stripe was left.

Someone claimed my prayers

snatched them
till they became gangly legs
a tattered hem
chased by bandits.

I wanted to grow a tree
count for something
more than penny wishes
slant.

Someone claimed my words
shook my elbows
till my voice fell
bruised in the grass.

What did I know of endurance
how shock waves subside
life can straddle a storm
spill open holy?

In the contemptuous midnight

the sky runs out of goodness
the sum of a house is want
the moon misreads luck
as a cesspool.

In the contemptuous midnight
the view from the bridge is sparse
the hotel for runaways holds no dream
my landlord speaks only the cadence of money.

In the contemptuous midnight
my bed is a rock field
stars jab the sky with a stick
every anonymous letter
that once called my name
holds inquest
answers with receipt.

You are weighing things

shoes, bodies, hours, bread
calibrations too loose or sticky.
I type a sentence
you count the syllables.
It is that kind of day.

The flame in my heart is ashen
wants to rise up fierce
keep a blaze.
Ice frosts the windows.

Once I thought I could
vouchsafe the sun
tack the moon to my table
ensure nothing goes missing

melt audacity
inside the swept clean
of my winter.

In the dark

sirens of the night speak
a language of haste, longing
as if abject places call our name
things get broken.

In the dark
stars sticker their face
onto my blue apron
my mother paws the bed
to bring back her lost lover.

In the dark
my anger holds seed
doesn't need to rework the meadow
drown the man in the splashy car
who knows nothing but smugness.

In the dark my spike heels
thud across cobbles
rub red the night's coarse eye
arrive at the harbor
where memory holds the hem of forgiveness
black waters beckon
the moon never needs
to beg for her splash pool.

In the territory of loss

I am knitting socks
knit knit knit
while the stove flames
the day aims to do better
move beyond this gaping hole
into a new landscape.

I am contemplating your shotguns
exits, entries
the brief of a life
how stories can muddy in fiction
fabricate a stage set, family
kiss as they kill.

Once I saw a woman fall out
of a twenty story building
and not splatter
like a seagull
she'd grown sturdy wings
barely grazed the concrete
then rose.

Can we always count on luck

carnations over a callous wind
the enunciation of meadow?

I have seen strangers speak
in a tongue that slaughters
dinner plates travel
between feast and famine
the day leak rust, innuendo, sumac
a half-sung death bed

have heard of those who rise
from their room
carry the host of the dark
everything
holy.

We had been courting

the time honored pasture
its bluegrass and jewelweed
lambs in the field
ponies

but then fire holds no allegiance
can take the hay, barn
roof, meadow
travel us to unimaginable places

where the burning woman
must rise on stilts
the two lovers are a memory
every bell tolls loss
carts off our voluptuous sunset.

Back then

did we look different
presentable
our pants a measure of decency
our shoes no continent of tears

did we carry ourselves with grace
among the matchsticks
sweep over the roads as if they
hold no dread
serpent tongue
shotguns?

Once were we tincture and dawn
the bright shooting star
your precious?

Still this schism
between where we begin
what we become.

Don't leave me here Pasha
wandering amid the nomads
selfish and blind.

Part Two

What does the Dark Dream

What does the dark dream

when it's a shaved room
peeled from the day's Cyprus
what does it say about rivers
the woman with rundown heels
who carries her home in a parcel

what does it say about celebrity
card playing
paradise on a shoestring

will it offer up a plate of potato
cure want of its sickbed?

We are picnicking

a Sunday in June.
My father's feet big, sweaty
when he takes off his sneakers
my mother's hair sheened auburn
the ants determined to climb onto
our pumpernickel bread, salami, chips.

We are picnicking as if the day needs us
no one will vanish from a cramped life
my father is not the juggler of three jobs
my brother won't end up a death note.

It is late afternoon.
The sun insistent in the sky.
Nobody has forecast that the modest
valley of our hopes will get snatched
some pain carries a landslide
nobody predicts too young
my mother will vanish
diligence guarantees nothing
in the Land of Oz.

When my children attempted to banish

the dark for looting
I called on the sky to save them
six safe words and a feather
since the dark is everybody's business
stirs itself into our soup
our coffee, marriage
conceits
causes eyes to shut
families to migrate.

When my children attempted to cull
the dark of its shade trees
I sent them to bed with no supper
the night being silent but loyal
willing to prod things
offer up more than treacle.

He calls me *flimsy*

as if I unravel too easy
am a breath of wind
with no spine
night of stars
only half stickered

speaks grown up
an avalanche of conceit
amid famine
where every hour hauls
a pearled voice
waxed words that threaten to protect
end up a bloodbath.

I watch him cut down
the forests
dissolve the dignity
of so many creatures
in the name of greed.

The man upstairs

on the double decker bus may or may not
know something about hope, endurance
may be dreaming a new job
the arms of his parent, lover, child
may wish he'd never been born
or else be reliving as we speak
the splash pool of his heart's seedbed

the man upstairs on the bus
may be watching the trees, the houses pass
shop windows, bus stops, pavement
may dream one day he will arrive at the ocean
white sand, a sunlit beach
that the world's uncertainties will come right.

The man upstairs on the bus moves slow
isn't about to run down the steps
call out the landlord for charging too much
doesn't always think his body looks decent.

He is clean shaven.
Has a windbreaker zipped over his shirt
brown shoes.
Is waiting for the stop on Sutter Street.
Won't tell you about his terminally ill wife
the way he counts coins careful
what day he was married, born, downsized.

At stop 75 steps off the bus
slowly walks the half block to his bread shop
bags a brown seeded loaf
wraps it careful
for the journey back.

The boy down the block

likes to drown things
spiders, ants, flies
likes lighter fluid
girls who shrink from swear words
follows them, taunts them
till they run.

The boy's father ammunitions
his house with rifles
keeps a locked safe
skins possum, rabbits.
Somewhere along the line
the mama went missing
but that was years ago
when the world trafficked in lilac
no cage held a pet.

The boy has hands the size of a ball mitt
can squeeze things till they bleed
doesn't yet know the true color of April
kisses that come unreserved
how out in the grass
the meadowlarks still memorize
his name.

When the birds came

flocks and flocks and flocks
swamped our carefully lit home
swept the lawn clean of seed
pawed the patio
with pale feathers and splat

when the birds came
unperturbed
dirtied our car, lampposts, swing set
as if the sky holds chaos
suburbia is no gem

when they stayed day after day
pecked the trees, pets, lawn furniture
vowed to stay close
we brought everything indoors
the sandbox, plastic flamingos
picnic table, barbecue
began to race from door to vehicle
keep our children away from
from their playground, bicycles

as if the world had turned hazardous
willing to smother us with wing, ransack
as if what was once ours was now theirs
and suddenly we were the leftovers
a stalked race.

I'd heard the queen of media talking

about her fifth hit in so many years
how the studio charts love her
and of course followers by the millions
who paint her neon
in the name of hype
heard about her irksome past
exercise regime, enviable health
ironed out wrinkles.

I'd heard about the queen of media
power of influencers
world of primp and receipt
men who tug at the dark, rip things
meadows split from their orange
about displaced people
extinct species
the earth warmed up as a cook stove
wasn't sure if I was alien or out of date.

Enquiry from the Rock Quarry Foundation

When the RQF wanted an interview
showed up at my door with their pen and paper
I was not sure what to say.
It is true basalt is different from gypsum
rock quarries have hazards all their own
the patron saint of stone evades pert answers

it is true my father died in the quarry accident
but that was years ago when precautions were thin
when his flask, the pail my mother packed
went forever missing

but it appears from talking to the two reps
that the real reason for their call is existence
whether I'll agree they still have a right to be here
mining the earth of its gem fields
whether the senator transplanted from Rhode Island
has a rod up his ass for circulating
a smear campaign over the quarry's safety.

They remind me that we can't live without rock
in fact even the bible says so
that the weakly build house
is a sloped tower of Pisa
foundations count.

When the men from the RQF began to test my patience
my mom being a widow for a dozen years
I had to consider how we live
the merits of firm ground
if we are intended to be a dust pit
suck up forests, animals, people
decent folks like my father
become voracious
a lack of repentance.

You are dealing cards

for rummy
dealing them out as if
queens and kings matter
every storybook prince
wants a home.

I have known you to be sly
hoard prize hands
in a cramped suitcase
then lay down a landslide.

You shuffle, fan like a pro
leave me wanting for scrap
a three piece set
pagan queen
orphaned ace.

I practiced my penmanship

curly cues, continent of commas
practiced my polite wishes
windstorms

but still the night trafficked in lost gulls
a sea of merchants
still my arms reached out for you
reached out.

If you come
please come empty
ready to receive me
not as the thrashing wave
but resonant
finally arrived back.

When the patron saint of invisible places

comes calling amid lock and keys
breaks down our door
for lack of answer
when the tapes of the past
no longer repeat and repeat
will it be easy to sponge death down
make it behave?

When the patriot of unearned places
eats down my forest
turns the sky black as an angry fist
will it be enough to count money
make the day into a stretch mat

will the seasons come right
be more than a fish gutted ocean
come to us plaintive
offer up a place for you, for me
at the table?

When the rain comes

the ground sops up
more than it knows
when words unfasten
finger the willow, grubs, roses
turn flimsy want into flame

then will you forgive
the way we court death
from a shrew plate

remind me of the lambs
stumbling yesterday in the field
the grocer who for free
bags me extra potatoes

the two mares at the fence
their dark eyes upon my face
patient, ever so patient
waiting for my hand to lift
gift them with apple.

He is counting up

my face
its sweetmeat and angles
sodden kisses
apostrophes

counting up my body's fire brigade
the precision of roses
aim his words like a rifle
while the patron saints watch.

He is counting up success stories
taking down every unworthy star
wants to ensure my derelict
goes missing.

Something courses through my life

that is more than diplomas, title, money
more than tidy kisses
the bush stripped bare

something comes to me
without want, pretense
soliloquies the dark
holds brightness and home
turns my ill-mannered girl into river.

It is November
snow dusts the trees.
Soon we will make our way
down the path to the pond
skate and skate in circles
as if the world knows peace
every stranger, tree, hill, fox
holds the language of blessing.

Who impels the sun

to bestow warmth
disavow rock throws
turns desire into daisies

who consoles the orphaned child
so that even amid concrete
the orange of sunset remains

who soft soothes the wind
parables want into a poem
impels the lame woman to lift

who drifts the music of rivers
soothes the cow, chicken, goat
coaxes the night sky to
send forth crystal

who eats at the table thankful
asks me to remember
the stolen field of poppies
that in the pearled valley
of my soul
still live?

Who climbs the trellis

of my heart
refuses to sit only
at the frothed table
asks the night to swell with no blade

who sups at the poor man's table
washes the walls
swabs the woman's stab wound
doesn't need to catalog pain
tame the dark
to keep the day safe

who turns lament into pasture
carries the child forth
to become full grown
an annotation of pear trees

who out of the hours of loss
coaxes the moon to stay loyal
sing to us
even in a blackened dress

who insures the meadow
still hums with bees
every album is a memory
lesson in roses?

Part Three

In the Country of my Longing

The plaudits of my heart

are a reckless sea
peopled with shells
the crush of wind
untimely arrival of newborns.

You carry kisses
wet as stones turned slick
by the tide's variance.

Once I was a caretaker
Inuit of unnamed places
tucked your salt on my tongue
slept with it

let you trespass
the bed of my sorrows
with your lips.

The hours

run on frayed seam
a petroglyph of roses
run on ransack and homily.

I want to find the gold egg
Jesus pin that never rusts
search the attic for answers.

For how many hours
has beauty worn clipped wings
the playhouse sat empty
for how many hours
have those dwarf kingdoms
called to me
offered up the promise
of more than attrition?

I am peeling things loose

the diabolical and mischief
hard parts and inertia
want to stroke till things come right
like the patron saint of everyday miracles
who takes the nearly departed
the overstuffed, tainted, unloved

turns them into more than
a measure of performance.

When the night comes
rattles my voice, past
amid a sky of flamethrowers
will I still believe
you are my one and only
steady creature in a sea of foam?

Listen.
The stars call out of vacancy.
The moon needs no throne.

My mother is wearing

dove feathers and sunset
a chronic smokestack
keeps her eye on me
as if I am meant to be more than pert
the girl tethered to eyeliner and plastic.

I have seen her go out with a stick
banish the man I've been dating
turn the rain into a pool
for her god's lips.

My mother is wearing the resin of cedar
table manners of forest
refuses to turn the earth skeletal

it is for her I write in this notebook
impel my heart not to rust.

I can imagine you

as the dead ringer
of someone I once loved
the apostle's first playmate
who slid away in a messy April
promised to come back
rinse the past of obsidian

can imagine you carrying water
the day not unlike this one
newborn sheep in the field
hours spread green
unperturbed

can imagine you bailing hay
handing me your unsoiled hanky
carrying a slice of god
in your pocket.

I want to see you tonight

cup my heart beneath your window
recite lines of Tsvetaeva
as if even the starved bird can sing
my voice is more than hurt
a boatload of longing.

I want to see you tonight
twirl in my dress
carry a slice of cake
in my yellowed napkin

bring you the spruce forest
washerwoman's singing
this slice of cake.

Let me remember you

as a coronation of birds
the nights' least steely homily
let me marvel at the places you've been
those trials bought and sold
way you've siphoned goodness
from a thin loaf

marvel at how you can live
in this muddied water
not flinch

rise up
in the right season
exquisite
the splayed open iris
avalanche of daffodils.

Who causes the cock to still

the greedy to give up their money
who stirs honey into the bathwater
excavates our discontents
till we are a speck of duff
riding the ocean

who unbinds the fox
shepherds the fallen flame
congregates with wolf, wasp, vole
impels us to contemplate
the true alphabet of wealth
why the girl in the pasted landscape
felt forced to turn pale?

If I woo you with poems

buttered toast, potato
will a seat arrive at the table
travel the territory of loss
the barbed words
axed prayer wheel?

When you come
will I strip naked
twine my lips
to the speech of birds?

In the country of my longing

fortune climbs a dwarf limb
turntable of patriots
blue black epistle

is the ruined friend stapled
to anonymous love notes.

In the country of my longing
I am more than scant
the girl in a torn dress

April arrives with narcissus
a punctuation of daisies.

What if fire drives the sledge

burnishes the wheels
turns the girl with steamy cologne
into more than an inferno
impetuous midnight?

Back then was she lovesick
unable to rid the field of its tyrants
in your hands did her past come clean
flame spell more than a deathbed
spell the risen commotion of roses?

The patron saint of fallen means

you appear at my breakfast table
your robe shabby
body the thin rail in a sea of angular
don't talk about loss
beg for scrap
lust over my potato and eggs

but still life holds a certain decency
mercy is asked to travel
with a steady thrum

for you I steep tea
set out plate
butter more toast
listen.

Was I awe struck

the day I met you
wordless
your soft face stilling
a culled landscape

was I awkward
less than you hoped
pedestrian or too touchy
inked in a messy scarlet
the shy creature
unsure what to say

could you understand my longing
that comes on a fragile wing
tempts being broken
when the day travels blind
not every kiss is a friend?

When I call your name

out of the damp moss
profusion of lilac
enter your body

will I find there
the shelter of finch
grace that washes
the feet of a stranger

or only the stoned wall
harsh refractory
words stoned to death
in a sordid country?

When you come to me
come simple
hinged to the language of birds
or not at all.

What will the night bring

of damp stars
the subterfuge of angels

will it stomp at my door
insist on a feast that is
more than callow rosebuds?

Will your birds conquer
an aberrant moon
shrink me
to fit inside your crystal?

Your dark is a shower of stars

festival of loss
luminous
while the trees sway.

I lick frost
thread the shy measure of your voice
into my coat seam
as if silence sanctifies.

In the headlamp of my heart
mythic deer keep wandering.

Part Four

A Mistress of Stolen Vows

I have heard

there is a canal
where lovers stall
on blue black water
boatman ferry
the night drowns in moist lips.

I have heard there is a place
with fish, many fish
where sheep doze
no one goes hungry.

You will know it
by a blind moon
plate of secrets.

When you come
I will be sitting in dust
by the side of the road
not empty of my past
but amber tinged
every true word
I have ever uttered
a burning for you.

Voices

I fold cheese, bread, gherkins
into a napkin
set off to find you
wherever you are.

The day carries water.
Carries water.
Unashamed the ghosts of the dark
come back to greet.

The phlox call my name.
The bread boxes of the dead sing.

Out back

the myrtle has grown thick
deer plunder the new
stalks of raspberry.

Is it possible April
will look away
see only want in my squat kitchen?

Every morning this reckoning
over what I've become
what it means to remain decent.

When the river calls
the sky relents of its grey
tell me I will unburden
my words, my body
come to you unabridged
a ceremony of kisses.

When I wear down my browns

my sepia tones
concave and elastic
will you grant me a small wish
that doesn't just spend and gamble
but feathers the meadow
holds things close

when I wear down my knobby
come to you with a different voice
will the stars snap free
pronounce me as more than
the one who weighs things
pronounce me soft?

It isn't the first time

you've knocked down my door
my loves
set the house on fire
kept me shambling
amid the gravestones

so why is it I still long
for what I can't explain
perch my ear to your forest
repentant?

If restlessness

grows a new purse
the riotous tides empty
what will you say

will my life be more than
an open wound
sodden raincoat

will my dress come right
words kneel once and for all
at your salt's table?

You carry the weight of sorrow

fledgling cosmos
the world indiscriminate
the world in waiting

my voice a stitch
travelogue
you have yet to enter.

It takes persistence to be here
mind the day
find the Abigail still alive
singing blind
from my backyard tree.

I bless your hands

that are blue ink married to
thin sheaves of paper
a cemetery of fallen kisses
books that spell loss
homecoming, detention

bless lovers who can nest death
place a stone in one hand
emptiness in the other

bless the country of lost souls
the patron saint of misfits
birds' insistence
territory of greed
dissolved in a corn field

bless your lips
that are half bluesy redemption
a door open to strangers

and as for the hours
the hours
they are less since I wait on you
and out of the darkness
you come.

In the notebook

of the patron saint of everyday miracles
I am more than biding time
waiting for the train
more than my salad sandwich
the even lines of a page

the street holds gulls, people, coffee
a boy in blue work shirt
woman carrying salt, potato, soup
buses that salute the trees as they pass

the street holds grass and worm
cardinal and cathedral
even the forgotten animals look up
hopeful.

In the notebook
of the patron saint of everyday miracles
snow arrives generous, buries the cars
the sirens of the dark hold cream
a kiss without forceps

my voice get hosed, hushed, canopied
the Sicilian baker smiles as I pass
as if we are all one of a kind
specks of wonder.

Who makes for beauty

tethers the child to the field
vouchsafes the meadow
insists swallows return
the earth offers up sunset

who stills the harsh wind
causes the old person to sing
the woman to slice tomato
for your toast
grind the coffee

who insures nothing goes missing
we are more than replaceable
that every fragile act
imperfect as it is
becomes the salt stained murmur
of you calling?

The night is a mistress of stolen vows

likes to rehearse
scratch at my door
as if the past knows no deathbed
my pond is seeded in fish eggs.

But when you come again
let it not be out of greed
the nuptial of knife blades
let it not be gentle then cruel

when you come
place your lips to my cheek
please carry the tulips of April
confetti of blossoming trees
a soft voice
that doesn't spew answers.

When the dark

spat at my face
accused me of absence
untimely remarks
a bench press

I began to coax with
the light's torn edge
Sunday school practice
girls who hold diligence
like a messy bride

began to coax
with feathered fetish, petals
an inaugural path to the well.

It is unclear what my life
will amount to
now that your serpent tongue
lays green eggs
among my willows.

I thought of you yesterday

inked lines on my arm
so I wouldn't forget

slept with your wind
that anoints my flint
with jasmine

slept with your lips
that are salt and siren
a longing for river

slept with your faith
that is part orchid
a host of cranes.

In the book of the patron saint of wonders

you remain the willing servant
load hauling ant
arctic cub on a shrinking planet
stay loyal to the sap of trees
river spawning salmon

no nightdress is too scant
the moon doesn't need
to take hostage.

In the book of the patron saint of wonders
the singed prayer holds psalm
the dark carries matchsticks
coneflowers lift.

It would be a mistake

to think I fell into the world
landed unscathed.
Things happen.
We prowl, puff, genuflect, waver.
But still the patron saint of wonder
casts out doubt
the shriveled bush grows back
the hummingbirds outlive
an historic heat wave.

You'd think by now I'd be
disavowed of miracles
ones that arrive on a sharp wing
promise you the world then flee
that the woman washing laundry
would tire of her hands' indenture
you'd think love was a sieve hole
moving on from one to the next

till the patron saint steps in
swallows our cramped notions
of success, celebrity
makes the trees wave
the leaves swirl pavement
the man on the bench tip his hat

makes for hope amid the street vendors
the downcast, broken
offers up a room, chair, hot plate.

See how you occupy my dark
take up a lot of legroom
bring tea, bread to the bare table.
Call to me unperturbed.

They are playing boules

something folks do
with time on their hands
a willing landscape.

I like to watch their excitement
over where the ball lands
the skill of a throw

like to imagine the world
could work like this
nothing too urgent
the maple trees in the park
twining March into new leaves
the ducks on the pond
a strut of feathers

the day not dispossessed
but precious.

This day

a conquest of petals
fused to the sky's blurred body.

How can I carry you as salt
lick my wants as they fly
remember you as more than
the unctuous word
night buried in tar pitch?

When you arrive
sweep the dust from my table
come unburdened
amber as the candle burning
the earth's repository of kisses
don't say I will turn away.

You persist

pretend to be my one and only
as if there is an assurance in
ring sets, handholding
not all circumstances
are provisional.

Will I stall in my tracks
turn you into the autumn groom
shiny lover
radiant
alive in my pocket?

When I come

carrying the limp bouquet
of a bygone era
salt stained, messy
practicing the words of the dead
unsure of the territory
what makes things sing

forgive me my espionage
need to press chords
out of the thinnest keys
forgive the homily of tyrants
way the earth gets hostaged
till midnight wears a thick veil

when I come
an encyclopedia of nothing
take all of me
canker and warts
sweetmeat and thistle
kisses preserved in a glass jar
and the ones that come loose
wild and free as the river.

Hear my plea

there is a place beyond here
you will know it by its abandoned well
the noisy sway of sugar patrons
muddied body of a woman
who once kept the world's time
according to her own heartbeat.

To know this place
you must carry salt
the wings of spring
damped down with rain.

I cast out my kisses

a poor woman in a sea of sticks
cast out my heart's angular
that sleeps in a blue forest

cast out my words with their
penchant for grievance
cast out the sun's bald head
the spittle of saints
when they're marking time
and want more

cast out my train wrecks
cadavers and cramped room
cast out the earth's flint
approximations of winter

till limp, almost forgotten
you came to me
in your petaled dress.

I tell you about my history

travel your body
sacrament the river's edge.

We are being loose, vagrant
as if life still holds a meadow
is more than peripatetic longing
a boatload of words.

I unfold my hankie
the one that holds the past
dead fish, a crimped landscape
turn it into cake
for the valley of your mouth.

Fashion me one of your nosegays

pivot and swing me
in your rope of a dress
paper wing my past
tilt your birds toward my porch
happy and free as the sunset

remind me of the vastness of children
roll call a hope that holds sturdy
come to me as a well
not pauper but friend

show me how to drink
from your cup
patient
a ceremony of petals.

When the merchants came

the do-gooders
the sweepers of pain
ambassadors of a spaceship

when the fields emptied
hills no longer rose and fell
pine trees gave up their wish list
razors began to camouflage as love
and love as a cesspool
when our kisses grew obstinate

I called out your name
crawled into the night's sleep sack
wept and slept
wept and slept

till my soul grew a pear tree
and the birds flew in
perched on the branches
and the insects came
and your hands
your hands that are fog and rain
vestibule and light
stargazing.

When the patron saint of miracles slips in

uninvited
rattles my illusions of an accomplished life
soup and bread always at the table
when things fall apart
my marriage, family, house, job

when I am forced to squat
fall through the cracks
accept my losses
the sunken bride in a sea of twigs

then will every cup of coffee
blade of grass
available bed
become precious
marry me to kisses
nobody owns?

When you arrive

amid our rally of thirst
city of merchants
pass your feet through the door
offer up magpie, prayer
your body's hymnal

when you arrive
press your lips
as an ancient friend
let me wipe clean
my voice at your table

come swept
self-possessed even
in an open bathrobe.

What can I say

about the diligence of wings
varied thrush, hummingbird's frenzy
determination of insects
way the fig tree refuses to forget
travels back beyond the ice field

what can I say about your body
its compilation of rivers
flirtation of cranes
how you practice the earth's precious
bow low

what can I say about my love
that arrives on a sad wind
stapled to autumn
the way your hands
carry water
splash me
from a paper cup?

No one said I was destined for aerial

but still the unpredictable happens
the ground moves away
I flap my arms
rise up and up and up
till the world takes on a new scent
less alien, inscrutable

up and up and up
till my mind grows sky
a hillside of maize
the cloud's handshake.

I tell you it is a different world
I became a bird amid birds
speck of the light's singing.

Part Five

Three Parts Flame

You are solar powered

my bright elixir
incurable meadow.

When the day upends
what will dissolution amount to
with my palette of poems
yellowed past
littered with heirlooms

now that you come to me
firm
irrevocable
plant your noble limbs
in my tree?

I'm not sure

I am marriage material
the comely bride
who waxes bright
holds painted nails
a muscular body
won't wane

not sure of the reasons
you want to marry me
broken branches
a desolation of night angels

but still this romp
through the field
still this annunciation
of springtime.

When we move from here

our hands hinged
to each other
around a common flame
spell our names
as more than loss
the pinched landscape
sing out your field
to the fiddle's refrain

when we move from here
the night come clean
angels roaming our forest

then will every small girl
fearful of getting snatched
be answered with cake?

You might think

the everlasting stays sane
a matter of bible study
formula and treatise
that the girl who lifts shoeless
has forgotten the penalties of flight

you might think the woman
wearing the finely carved cameo
belongs to an antique past
territory of fiction
might have a room of opinions
this being the age of answers

but then strange things happen
the sun peels my orange
ordinary sack cloth, slogans
turn into the patron saint's daybook
a lounge chair of lupine.

You came to me

in the fallow season
when crops slur
the rain holds a drumbeat
crocus are left
to reimagine spring

came to me
when my wants were thin
worship wore a tattered veil
came to me
with your armload of bird pecks.

How could I refuse
such bread at the table
meet you with less
when the folds of my dress
kept lifting?

You are crushing cardamom

for the dinner
as if it has another life to give
an aromatic way of saying *holy*.
All afternoon loss has traveled me
like a hurt dog.

But you wait
patient soul of the universe
slice ginger, garlic
as if I am more than sodden
the down on my luck
hapless bride.

You are crushing cardamom
sing under your breath.
Is it for this the sky flirts
the sun splashes my terrace
with petals?

Year after year

I have come to your piano
tried to tame my fingers
into something more than
slippery roads, a ship wreck
impelled them to loosen
sink into the keys
find something.

It has been a slow journey
giving up what I know
in the name of your heart's
unfettered wade pool.

Chords drift in
the scent of lilac
flutter of finch
weight of the world's tears
hush of an angel's lament
I translate into you.

Without fork or spoon

condiments or censor
I come to your table
let my hands lead
be your generous saltshaker

break up bits of bread
cheese, radish
for your mouth.

Now that the mineshafts
my cramped days have fled
you traffic in phlox
lay extra green eggs
amidst my willows.

In the patron saint's daybook

the ink blurts blue
words stumble, reignite
there's a smudged lotus
river with wrinkles
lost saints
tilted tower of Pisa
girl crowding the wealth of petals
into her pocket.

In the patron saint's daybook
the past is a cross stitch of vows
first kiss
the third eye of the moon weeping
I am more than anonymous
remain the holy persistence
of your pear trees.

On a clear day, at a certain hour

the voices of the saints rise up
not for the sake of a cold beer
pocket of change, news pitch
not to measure the tomatoes
weight of a face's wrinkles

but to wonder who felled the trees
laid concrete over the poppies
delivered dead roses in a bridal basket.

On a clear day, at a certain hour
the voices of the saints rise up
wake the dead from their sleep
as if the world might end tomorrow
we are fated to be more.

When your shoes rise out of the closet

be ready
not every romance is rooted
not every periled thought
needs a light bulb

geese flap before they fly
turn south seeded by instinct

don't fear your lips magnum
kiss the dust, the birds
the sky, the sun
as you lift.

When you peek into your soul

ponder its width
latitudes of wing and weight
unravel the dross

don't expect only luminous
fish to pool
tyrants to forever vanish

go deep
plum the avenues
of your forest
mind the birds
mind the birds.

When I worship you

wipe my fingers in your honey
let it stand for something more than
the tyrant queen with a headset
men who must shout
concrete the world blind

when I worship you
slip my willing ear to your worm hole
let it be out of a sodden place
my life in a slush pile
mind empty of dross.

When I arrive inside

the sermon of hope
dig scum off my shoes
smooth down my dress
the world's tangles
when I arrive coin-less
the past being the past
and sometimes gruesome

it can feel right
to unburden my lips
offer up homage
sooth the sky's rock field
the body's hinged breath

spell content out of the forest
bend our hailstorms
into psalm.

Have you come

pecked a hole in my jacket
carved room for the rain's diligence
the unruly sun
child's forage for mealtime

have you arrived
on a shy wind
not to take from the earth
but to give to it

your hands a merchant of plums
your voice bare
as the hollowed trees?

Listen

when the stars run
their unruly fingers

through the hair of my sky
I want to be ready

pick their lint
off the ground
luminous.

To eat cake with a saint

takes more than good manners
wiping the lips nice
the apprenticeship of paisley
fantasy lovers speckling
the forest.

To eat cake with a saint
takes slow time
no quarrel over minefields
every shooting star a gift
letting them pilfer your pockets
plant what they want
not resist.

When the cottonwoods arrived

they were flush with life
offered their homecoming
as if the patron saint of miracles
doesn't prioritize importance
prop some things on a pedestal
while others perish.

The cottonwoods welcomed
the swallows
squirrels, ants, beetles
the rain, snow
the light, shade
the opulent
the ditches
the left out
the lost.

We have seen the glow

almost phosphorous
the way it cups children
turns hearts, hands
luminous
soft hues the grass
weathered barn

have seen the glow
at first a hint from the distance
then nearer and nearer
up close

till the muddy roads, bent ones
don't much matter
till we need glasses
to temper the glare
so much brightness.

We have seen the glow
call it equinox or morning star
call it being buried in light
then suddenly
this surplus of singing.

Today the patron saint of favors arrived

offered up a handful of snap peas
as if the earth wants to please
and the farmer's hand
and the sun married to seed
and the rain that cracks us open
till we sprout.

I snipped off the ends
one by one ate them
as if the patron saint of favors
speaks in the name of love
in the language of snap pea.

They say it takes centuries

to birth a new planet
prop it up, people it
with fox, river, meadow, kindness
that might is a thin sword
in a country of ambush.

I have been scraping off beauty
its rust and cankers
this being July
the month of my birth
the weather exuberant
a season of bright lit answers

my this and thats in decay
every blade of grass
flower a talisman
my lips wanting to spill
a flood of fireflies
for you.

Now that the wind has hushed

the field lays littered with kisses
my past seeps a pond
sweet grass, rosemary

now in this valley of fruit trees
how can I squeeze want
into my bathrobe
when I have found you?

Maybe

life doesn't always listen
grow conciliatory
but still this quiet festival
amid the roses
the rise up of kale
rhubarb, spinach

still this faith of sunrise
birds that travel me
peck clean my breath
as they fly.

We called into the future

fed it an olive branch
bandaged midnight
cashed in our stolen shoes
till out of the forest
you came
amber with sunrise.

Now my dress blazes
I am the sum of lips
in a flood of poppies.

We cut the ribbon

clip, clip, clip
dancing girl in her twig dress.

See how the day misbehaves
the field inks scarlet
my hair carries misdemeanors
a seedbed

see how every word
I have ever spoken
has finally turned
into grass.

Color blind this love

still the tulips punctuate
the camellias approach
in their flirt dress

but gone the sorting
the shifting
the dribbles of mercy
that wear a tight fit.

Pasha

I am carrying out
bread and goat cheese
one yellow bud

my heart
that is three parts flame
a fistful of sand

carrying out to you
my shrunken words
bare feet

and bells
so many bells.

In the field

the sheep, two horses
know me
pause their munching
to watch as I pass

and is it not for this
that the wind sings
the grass fingers holy

that beyond all trespass
barriers
creature to creature
we share this earth
in strangeness
in faith?

Toni Thomas lives in Portland, Oregon. Her poems have been published in Austria, Spain, New Zealand, Canada, England, Scotland, and Australia. In the United States her work has appeared in over fifty literary magazines including *Prairie Schooner, North Dakota Quarterly, Hayden's Ferry Review, the Minnesota Review, Notre Dame Review, Poetry East*, and more. She has been twice nominated for a Pushcart prize, and won several awards. She has published twenty-seven collections of poetry and six books for children.

Her figurative clay sculptures have been shown in gallery exhibits in Portland and Chicago, displayed in literary magazines, and housed in private collections in the U.S. and England.

Her short documentary *One of Us* was shown at the Trans-ideology: Nostalgia festival in Berlin and at the Museum of Contemporary Art in Taipei.

Since Toni loves to create and sits buried in reams of poems, manuscripts, clay figures and images….she likes to imagine all of them out in the world swaying wild as the lupine.

tonithomaspoetry.com

www.ingramcontent.com/pod-product-compliance
Lightning Source LLC
Chambersburg PA
CBHW020341010526
44119CB00048B/555